THE **CRAZY** WORLD **OF**

BOWLS

CARTOONS BY

Bilstatt

EXLEY
NEW YORK • WATFORD, UK

Other cartoon giftbooks in this series:
The Crazy World of Cats (Bill Stott)
The Crazy World of Football (Bill Stott)
The Crazy World of Gardening (Bill Stott)
The Crazy World of Golf (Mike Scott)
The Crazy World of Housework (Bill Stott)
The Crazy World of Marriage (Bill Stott)
The Crazy World of Rugby (Bill Stott)
The Crazy World of Sex (Bill Stott)

Published simultaneously in 1997 by Exley Publications LLC in the USA,
and Exley Publications Ltd in Great Britain.

12 11 10 9 8 7 6 5 4 3 2 1

Copyright © Bill Stott, 1997

ISBN 1-85015-939-4

Printed in China.

Exley Publications Ltd, 16 Chalk Hill, Watford, Herts, WD1 4BN, United Kingdom.
Exley Publications LLC, 232 Madison Avenue, Suite 1206, NY 10016, USA.

"I'm getting jut a bit fed up of you re-living the deciding end, Gordon...."

"I'm pleased he's got a hobby – I just wish he wouldn't use the adjoining wall!"

"'Course I don't just live for bowls. There's er.... Then, there's... er... er...."

"Look! A blue bit!"

"So, you're quite keen on bowls are you, Henry?"

"That's the Wilkinsons. Identical track suits, caps, bags – and oddly enough, they're just as bad as each other at bowls...."

"So, we came to the final end, and talk about nip and tuck, I'll tell you, my heart was in my mouth. Then young Carl Phillips says to me, he says...."

"Hello Mrs. Jones... 'is back's gone again...."

"Sorry about that... trying out a new overarm delivery... hand slipped...."

"For really important matches, I can never decide which set to use."

"We were expecting a tough match, but this is ridiculous...."

"Whoops!"

"'Course as a new member you weren't to know that big Hilda always crushes a couple of bowls before a match. Unnerves the opposition, she reckons...."

"New to it is he? We don't often see a run-up...."

"Yes, yes... worms. We're bound to get the odd one. Calm down...."

"Ignore it. They're just trying to psyche you out...."

NEANDERTHAL BOWLS

"I know, I know! My wife's better than me – and I hate it! D'you hear? I hate it!"

"Right – nearest the jack or you're sawdust, pal."

"I don't like the look of this...."

"Don't be alarmed – it's traditional that the Fairfield match always starts with a brawl...."

"A bit keen, the opposition...."

"He usually starts from here when he's having a practice. We've only got a
short back garden...."

"There's nothing wrong with saying 'hard luck' – but you'll <u>have</u> to
learn not to snigger...."

"Superglue on the jack is just not funny any more, Ted...."

I know we're not an ageist club. I know she's good, but she's playing
havoc with the older members' nerves...."

"I'm all for bringing bowls to the country's youth, but is Gordon the right ambassador?"

"Leaves nothing to chance, your partner?"

"I'd just like to remind you that there is a time limit in league matches...."

"'Course since the game's made it big on T.V., Bernard's insisting on make-up before each end...."

"He's such a bighead – but don't worry – there isn't a cassette in it!"

"Nothing like a bit of friendly rivalry."

"Uh uh – Hell's bowlers!"

"It's his own fault – the doctor's warned him about overuse of the forehand."

"Which reminds me, Jerry – how's the floodlights fund coming along?"

"I know they're two leagues below us, but try not to be so casual...."

"Well... I've seen better...."

"... can't stand folk who show off when they're winning...."

"The old stand was never built to take a Mexican wave...."

"Why don't you buy a case for them like everyone else?"

"For Heaven's sake, Muriel – we need the jack!"

"Typical, isn't it – taught her all I know, now, she's ten times better than <u>me</u>!"

"Personally, I think it's a great shame the senior member of the team doesn't like the new strip!"

"Will you stop panicking! Hardacre's not developed a new technique.
He's just had a hernia operation!"

"Funny how she always manages to faint during her last end."

"I see Charlie Fairclough didn't win the championship again this year...."

"Proposing? Don't be silly – he's having a practice...."

"Why can't you be like normal lottery winners and buy flash cars and world cruises?"

"Yes, they <u>are</u> just kids. Yes, they <u>are</u> muscling in our game... and yes, they did beat us!"

"It's the local news channel wanting to know how you're coping with defeat after the Windyridge bowls final...."

"And to cousin Derek, I leave my unique collection of bowls...."

"Hello Darling. Did you win?"

Books in the "Crazy World" series
($4.99 £2.50 paperback)

The Crazy World of Aerobics
The Crazy World of Hospitals
The Crazy World of The Office
The Crazy World of Sailing
The Crazy World of School

The following titles in this series are available
in paperback and also in a full colour mini
hardback edition ($6.99 £3.99)

The Crazy World of Bowls
The Crazy World of Cats
The Crazy World of Football
The Crazy World of Gardening
The Crazy World of Golf
The Crazy World of Housework
The Crazy World of Marriage
The Crazy World of Rugby
The Crazy World of Sex

Books in the "Fanatic's Guide" series
($4.99 £2.50 paperback)

The **Fanatic's Guides** are perfect presents for
everyone with a hobby that has got out of hand.
Eighty pages of hilarious black and white
cartoons by Roland Fiddy.

The Fanatic's Guide to Dogs
The Fanatic's Guide to Money
The Fanatic's Guide to Sports

The following titles in this series are available in
paperback and also in a full colour mini
hardback edition ($6.99 £3.99)

The Fanatic's Guide to Cats
The Fanatic's Guide to Computers
The Fanatic's Guide to Dads
The Fanatic's Guide to D.I.Y.
The Fanatic's Guide to Golf
The Fanatic's Guide to Husbands
The Fanatic's Guide to Love
The Fanatic's Guide to Sex